CALLED TO CHOSEN
The Process

Shardell Martin

Copyright © 2019 by **Shardell Martin**

All rights reserved. No part of this publication may be reproduced by any means, graphics, electronic, or mechanical, including photocopying, recording, taping, or by any information storage retrieval system without the written permission of the publisher except in the case of brief quotations embodied in critical articles and reviews.

Shardell Martin/Rejoice Essential Publishing
PO BOX 512
Effingham, SC 29541
www.republishing.org

Unless otherwise indicated, scripture is taken from the King James Version.

Called To Chosen/ Shardell Martin
ISBN-10: 1-946756-50-4
ISBN-13: 978-1-946756-50-3
Library of Congress Control Number:2019934571

DEDICATION

I thank you Lord that You are giving me the grace to recognize that You are speaking to me. Whether it is Your voice, Your word, blessing me with Your thoughts, ideas, or just allowing me to see and know Your ways. I truly believe and know that without You, I am nothing. Everything that I am able to do is because You strengthened and graced me to do it.

I am thankful for this journey You have allowed me to travel thus far. Although, there has been bumps, bruises, detours, delays, hurt, pain and a lot of suffering, I still would not trade this experience for anything. Neither would I want to go through it again. Most importantly, I am learning to accept and appreciate my process in spite of how it feels or seems because I know embracing it will and is making me better.

I am looking forward to continuing on this journey called life because I have You, my Heavenly Father.

So, thank you Lord for not giving up on me even when I gave up on myself.

To all who will read this book, ask the Lord to open your heart, mind and soul to receive and apply all that the Heavenly Father has to speak to you in Jesus' name.

Heavenly Father, in the name of Jesus, I pray that you touch everyone whose eyes will lay upon this book. Draw them that they may hear what your Spirit wants to speak to them. Bring forth clarity, understanding, healing, divine interruptions, set free, deliver, bring to repentance, and most importantly, a closer relationship with You. I decree and I declare divine alignment and agreement with the Word and Spirit of God that will usher them into divine purpose and destiny in Jesus' name. I pray they will experience You in an awesome and new way that will lead to You having the preeminence in their lives in Jesus' name. Amen.

TABLE OF CONTENTS

FOREWORD..xi

ACKNOWLEDGMENTS................................xiii

Chapter 1:   Opening of Your Eyes..........1

Chapter 2:   Sanctifying You...................7

Chapter 3:   Empty You Out.................13

Chapter 4:   Pouring Into You...............22

Chapter 5:   Intimacy............................28

Chapter 6:   Learning What God
               Requires of You...............38

Chapter 7:   Knowing Who You Are.....53

Chapter 8:   Walking In Who
               You Are............................62

Chapter 9:   Level of Sanctification
               And Requirements.............71

Chapter 10:	Going Higher.....................76
Chapter 11:	The Original You................81
Chapter 12:	Repeat..............................87

ABOUT THE AUTHOR...................................91

REFERENCES...93

FOREWORD

My name is Shakila Kendall. Author Shardell Martin is my sister in the natural as well as my Spiritual Leader who has been ordained by God. The impact that God has allowed the Woman of God to have on my life is indescribable. When you hear the word Christian, there are already certain expectations you have of someone. This woman has exceeded those expectations through trials, tribulations, the Grace of God and The Process. When I think of her, I think of the term "Disciple of Christ" and not just Christian. Her relationship with God is a lifestyle and not just a Sunday morning kind of thing. The Spirit of God truly dwells in her. That is why God has authorized her to share some enlightenment concerning The Process we have to go through as believers.

Although everyone's walk with God is different, we can all relate in some way and help each other through The Process which is exactly what this book will do. It will help you develop into a mature place and cause you to have a certain stature with God. No matter where you are at in your relationship with God, this book is for you. Many times, we get to a place in God and think "we have arrived." In this place, we need to be taught all over again. God will perfect us until the day of Jesus return. Therefore, when you are reading this book, be in tune to what the Spirit of God is speaking to you as an individual. Anyone who cross paths with Shardell will tell you the profound impact God has used her to make on their life and their relationship with God. May you have an ear to hear what the Spirit of the Lord is saying. Enjoy and Grow in the Grace and Knowledge of God!!!

Shakila Kendall

ACKNOWLEDGEMENTS

My Uncle Will- you were the start of my process when God used you that night to not only invite me to Service but take me. Not knowing that my life would be changed forever by God saving me, filling me with His Holy Spirit, and giving me a new start.

(The late) Bishop and Pastor Lee- God used both of your servanthood to start my journey/life of faith. I'm grateful for God using you two to impart, teach me about faith, obedience, prayer, and more. Thanks for being my first spiritual leaders!

Prophetess Kim – It was you God used to spark my interest in Prophets. You were a big spiritual support to me in my beginning years in Christ. God used you to help me in more ways than you know. Being able to come to you for counsel, prayer, and more helped me to keep going. Thank you.

Apostle Philip Green- You were the one God used to disciple me and introduce me to a God that was beyond what I was used to.

Mom- I thank you for all the support you offered me and my kids over the years. Thank you.

Apostle Carolyn Mcneil -Thank you for allowing God to use you to impart and activate the prophetic in me.

Ronder Butler- Thank you for allowing God to use you to house me and my children during a tragic and trying season.

To My Sister - Wow, It's so much I could say to you, but I will say this: I love you in a special way; you're more than just a sister to me. I would love if there were more sisters like you that way people would be able to experience and know the blessing you are and have been to me and my kids. Thank you for loving me the way you love me. Don't ever stop, nor stop being who God purposed you to be in my life because I need you.

My Kids- You two endured the sacrifice and suffering I had to go through in order to live out the call of God for my life. You two suffered through it with me. I love you all more than you all know. Having you all in my life changed me and my life for the better. When you all get older, you all will be able to look back and be grateful for what we had to go through because the fruit will speak for itself and nothing was in vain.

CHAPTER 1

OPENING OF YOUR EYES

Since August 2011, God has been directing and dealing with me through the lifestyle of Abraham. Many know Abraham as being the father of many nations, but I am learning that He is much more than that. Many do not realize God used Abraham to be the forerunner or one of the first to live a lifestyle of faith. Abraham believed God, and it was imputed or counted unto him for righteousness (Romans 4:3). This is why the just shall live by faith (Romans 1:17) because without faith it is impossible to please God (Hebrews 11:6).

We as believers have deviated so far from the lifestyle God wants us to live. This is why I say this, "God called Abraham alone to prepare him for the lifestyle He had purposed for him." Jesus said, "Sanctify them through thy truth thy word is truth (John 17:17)." How can one be ready for the purpose God has for them if they have not been sanctified through God's Truth first? For someone to be sanctified by God's truth one has to live according to the Word of God.

Sanctify: Set apart as or declare holy. To set apart for sacred use: to make holy; purify.[1]

AN ACT OF FAITH

God called me to come from the church that I was fellowshipping with. Not knowing what the outcome would be, I still took that step of faith, even when others disagreed with it. I know other people looked at it as being crazy because God was not calling me to go to a church but to a man who also was called to the sanctification process. Several weeks before meeting him, God allowed me to see how I was not following truth. Yet, at the time when God allowed me to see this, I did not realize that I was not following truth. I just knew things were not right. Jesus said we should go on and do greater works than He did (John 14:12), and that was not happening at the church I was at.

As I began to seek God out on my own, He brought to my attention a certain man of God. Out of everything I heard Him teach, God allowed me to focus on a particular scripture that he spoke. This scripture spoke to my Spirit, it was Matthew 6:33 which says, "Seek ye first the kingdom of God and His righteousness and these things shall be added to you." When I heard that Scripture, it literally revolutionized my life. It was like my Spirit quickened or came alive. Afterwards, my search began. I wanted to know everything that I could learn about the Kingdom of God. That is when God led me to my new teacher. My hunger for God began to be filled. As I was being taught, I remember feeling upset and tricked because I believed I was doing what I was supposed to do. Little did I know, I was following lies at the time. That hurt me but because of the Lord's grace it did not stop me from wanting God.

So, I continued fellowshipping with my new teacher who is an Apostle. This was the man God sent to disciple me and lay a foundation of the word of God in me. One Sunday during a revival service at my old church at that time, is when I made my mind up to follow God and I left. I remembered that next Sunday feeling like I needed to go to church because I was used to going every Sunday. So, I went to a nearby church. When I attended, I liked it. Plus, I remember hearing the pastor talk about the Kingdom of God, so I took that as a sign that this might be the place God wanted me to join. I attended the same church that following Sunday, and I felt nothing. After leaving and seeking Godly counsel, I realized God already sent who He wanted to teach me. A week after meeting him and hearing his teachings, I wanted him to come to my house so he could teach my mom, sister and brother. When he did, God showed up right in my house because the word of God says in Matthew 18:20, "When two or three are gathered in my name, I'm in the midst."

As a result, my mom rededicated her life back to God, which was a prophecy fulfilled. My brother also rededicated his life and my sister got an impartation from the Holy Ghost. A week later, my teacher and I were fellowshipping which I enjoyed because the Spirit of God was always showing up and I was being taught the truth of God's word. It was during one of our fellowships when God told me to tell him to start a bible study. He also told me to support him, so we did what God said to do. At the time, I was still spiritually immature because I didn't know or understand what God really wanted from me. I could not understand or see what God was saying to me. That is why I felt the need to continue attending church on Sundays. Most of the time we get used to doing things out of habit and not because we are being led of God's Spirit.

So, God made it clear to me that I was to submit to the Apostle's leadership. At that time, I still did not know how to make sense of it or understand it, but I continued in what God said to do anyway. I learned there were a lot of habits God had to destroy in me, so I can learn how to follow the Holy Spirit and not what I felt, thought, or what I was used to or comfortable with. God was preparing me for something, but at that time I did not realize what it was.

ENDING CONCLUSION: "WHERE I WENT WRONG."

Although God was leading me into the New, I allowed what I was familiar with which was the old and the things I was used to, to interfere with the leadership of the Holy Ghost and my obedience to God's word.

WHAT I LEARNED:

I learned that I cannot allow what I feel or think to override my obedience to God's word or leading of the Holy Spirit. We as believers have reduced God to be a God of what we feel, think, and are familiar with. I charge everyone who is reading this book to allow God to remove the blinders from your eyes, accept, and embrace what God shows you without making excuses. Just let God lead you beyond yourself and what you grew accustomed too. Yes, it is not going to make sense to you, and you will not understand at first, but God wants you to trust and believe Him. It may not make sense sometimes but this is real faith.

CHAPTER 2

SANCTIFYING YOU

Sanctify: set apart as or declare holy; consecrate. Free from sin; purify.[1]

Shortly after leaving the church that I was at, God directed me to the lifestyle of Abraham. After reading the 12th chapter of Genesis, it was made clear to me why I had to leave that church. Just as God called Abraham to be alone with Him, He was calling me in the same way as well. The persecution that I was experiencing was a reflection and a reminder to me that people and believers do not know God as much as they proclaim to. Their ignorance pushed me closer to following God and accepting my season of being alone. As I continued in being taught and seeking God in my personal time, He continued me in the sanctification process. It was not a pretty process.

In the sanctification process, God disconnects you from everything and everyone that you are familiar with. In Genesis 12:1, God told Abraham, whose name was Abram at the time, to leave his family, home, the land he grew up in and go to a place that He will show him. Anyone God has called or chosen to do a work for Him is going to go through a sanctification process; it is a must if you want to be an honorable vessel before God.

Nevertheless the foundation of God standeth sure, having this seal, The Lord knoweth them that are his. And, let every one that nameth the name of Christ depart from iniquity. But in a great house there are not only vessels of gold and of silver, but also of wood and of earth; and some to honour, and some to dishonour. If a man therefore purge himself from these, he shall be a vessel unto honour, sanctified, and meet for the master's use, and prepared unto every good work. — 2 Timothy 2:19-21

There are many examples in the bible of people that went through their sanctification process.

1. David

When he left his father to serve King Saul. Also, when David was on the run from Saul.

2. Elisha

After Elijah put his mantle on him, he made his parents one last meal. Afterwards, he followed Elijah. We also see some examples in the New Testament.

3. The twelve disciples

When Jesus picked his 12 disciples, they all had to leave what they were doing to follow Him.

Know that your sanctification process is needed to make you ready for the work God wants you to do. It is just like when you apply for a job, they tell you the list of qualifications that are needed to do the job. The same goes with God except you do not apply, He picks you, and He is the boss. Even if you have been in church all of your life or been saved for years, God still wants to take you through your sanctification process. Most of us will go through it more than once because we are not or have not been obedient to the process. If you are like me, you were in the process and/or completed the process but became contaminated during or after the work. Some may feel they do not need it because they have been saved for a while and they are doing the work but understand this, if God is not your number one influence then you need it.

And he is the head of the body, the church: who is the beginning, the firstborn from the dead; that in all things he might have the preeminence.—Colossians 1:18

If you consider the life of Joseph, how he grew up under his father, Jacob, who was a righteous man, but God still separated him from his father so He could raise Joseph up and be the number one influence in his life. If you are anything like Joseph who has been given a dream by God; a dream showing you your future and it has not come to pass yet. And in fact, your life is the opposite of what God has shown you. I want you to lift your hands up and tell God thank you because you are in your process. What God has shown you will come to pass. You are being blinded by what you see, hear, feel, do not have, and what has not happened yet. I was in that place too, and I had to make a choice either to trust God and walk by faith or to die spiritually or naturally in my wilderness. Let me encourage you to praise God even more because things are not what they seem. Your faith is being tested. Just as Joseph was thrown in the pit then sold off to be a slave, it was a part of his process to bring him closer to what God had for him and wanted him to do. You need to know that what people meant for evil God meant it for your good (Genesis 50:20). Therefore, embrace your sanctification process because it is bringing you closer to God and making you better in the process.

ENDING CONCLUSION: "WHERE I WENT WRONG."

I did not seek God for understanding during my sanctification process which caused me to make a lot of unnecessary mistakes. Like for example, God was giving me a lot of revelation through reading His Word. I would share it with my teacher at that time and he would challenge and question it. Because I trusted him, I allowed my teacher's voice to become more dominant for me than God's voice. He became the one I look to for understanding verses me going to God. Another mistake I repeatedly made was not being still long enough for God to give me the clarity on what He was saying to me whether it was Him speaking to my Spirit, through my dreams, people or His word. I was immature in understanding how God spoke to me.

WHAT I LEARNED:

One of the most important things I learned is if you become too reliant upon man or things, you can make someone or think they're God without being aware of it. God will allow friction and hardship between you and that person to teach you that He is your only God. I also learned and know that you have to sit still or seek God long enough to allow Him to make clear what He is saying to you. Do not lean to your own understanding. Most importantly, watch who you share information with. Just because God reveals or speak something to you doesn't mean it is for you to share. Some things He wants you to keep between you and Him and if there comes an appointed time to reveal what He has given you then, and then only should you release it. Remember, God is not revealing and speaking to everybody what He gives to you, so protect it.

CHAPTER 3

EMPTY YOU OUT

Empty: containing nothing, not filled or occupied.[2]

After God sanctifies you, there is still more work to be done. This work of emptying you out, is like all the rest, a constant work until Christ comes back.

Being confident of this very thing that he which have begun a good work in you will perform it until the day of Jesus Christ— Philippians 1:6

The reason why is because we are constantly being tested and tried by God. Whether we pass or fail, there is going to be something added or subtracted from us. For example, what if God is testing you on your submission to leadership or authority. I will show you three different scenarios. Let's examine the 1st scenario which is someone passing the test.

Consider this, in the season or time of being tested, you submitted yourself to authority or your leadership. As a result, you experienced being mishandled or treated harshly that lead to your feelings being hurt. Some people also experienced leadership who abused their authority to the point they controlled them vs. leading them. What I mean is that you need their permission for everything. If you wanted to visit another church, you must ask their permission or let them know. If someone asks you to preach at their church, you have to get the leadership's permission. These are some examples of control vs. leading.

So you abided by all their rules and when the season of being tested and submitting to authority or leadership is up, you hear God say, "You passed the test," despite the difficult. During the trial you got hurt from the way you were treated, bad impartations, and controlled vs. being led. Your perception of authority or leadership ended up being unhealthy or tainted because of the bad example and the rest of the things you suffered whether you faced humiliation, or feared leadership vs. respected them. Most importantly, they became your God.

In the 2nd scenario, again you are being tested in your submission to leadership but this time the results are that you failed the test. The following are examples of why you failed. You rebelled every time you were confronted or challenged by leadership. Whether it was the way you responded when you were asked to do something you did not like, or how you walked away from facing the problem. You just did not want to deal with it. They asked you to do something, and you did not do it. You argued with them. You wouldn't serve them. You neglected the responsibility you were given. Consider this, you did what they asked you to do in action but in your heart you did it with the wrong motive or intention.

Motive can be defined as a reason for doing something especially one that is hidden.[3] Intention can be defined as a thing intended; an aim or plan. It can also be defined as a determination to act in a certain way: resolve.[4] Examples of having the wrong motive or intention is when you do things to get on your leader's good side, manipulation, deceit, wanting to be seen, for position, favoritism, or recognition. You aren't doing things because you want to please God, being obedient, or along those lines.

In the 3rd scenario you are being tested in your submission to God, His word, and the Holy Spirit vs. your leader. This scenario has four different examples. The first example is that you are in a situation where God tells you to evangelize, and He starts dealing with you concerning it. However, your leader tells you that you are not ready yet. Who do you obey?

The second example, someone invites you to their church to preach. You pray on it. God says yes, but your leader says no. Who do you obey? The third example, you are on your way to Sunday service and you are in a leadership position. You leave the house in just enough time to make it on time because you have stern leadership who does not tolerate his or her leaders being late. However, the Holy Spirit is leading you to stop and feed someone or direct you to go somewhere else, who do you obey? The last example, the word of God teaches you to turn the other cheek, but your leadership teaches if someone hits you then hit them back because you are not there yet or God will forgive you. Who do you obey? In this last scenario of being tested, you were presented with four different examples which all ended in the question of who will you obey? If this has not happened to you, then it will because God tests us all in this way even Jesus.

If you are like me, then you have experienced all three scenarios; passing the test but still needing deliverance. Failing the test and having to repeat it again until I passed. I was also tested to see whether I would obey my leader over God, His word, and the Holy Spirit. Understand that God tests us to show us what is in us. His ultimate result for us is to be conformed to the image of His son Jesus.

For whom he did foreknow, he also did predestinate to become conformed to the image of his son, that he might be the firstborn among many brethren.—Romans 8:29

God wants to know if we will keep, follow, and obey His word which is Jesus.

And thou shalt remember all the way which the Lord thy God led thee these forty years in the wilderness, to humble thee, and to prove thee, to know what was in thine heart, whether thou wouldest keep his commandments, or no. And he humbled thee, and suffered thee to hunger, and fed thee with manna, which thou knewest not, neither did thy fathers know; that he might make thee know that man doth not live by bread only, but by every word that proceedeth out of the mouth of the Lord doth man live. — Deuteronomy 8:2-3

The 1st Scenario was the example of someone passing the test but there were some subtracting and adding that needed to be done. God would have to take away the hurt, bitterness, unforgiveness, wrong perception, negative mindset and anything else that would cause a person to behave opposite of the fruit of His Spirit.

But the fruit of the Spirit is love, joy, peace, long-suffering, gentleness, goodness, faith, Meekness, temperance: against such there is no law. — Galatians 5:22-23

Although I mentioned God adding and subtracting from us to make us better in this chapter, I will only deal with the things He subtracts because this chapter deals with being emptied out. In the next chapter I will talk about the things He adds.

The 2nd scenario was the example of someone failing the test. Understand when it comes to God you have to do things His way. There are no skipping steps of the process. This is why He will allow us to keep taking the same test until we pass. God will not put His stamp of approval on something undone. Even the children of Israel had to stay in the wilderness until they allowed God to complete the work that needed to be done. He does the same thing with us. Most of us have this form of Godliness but denied the power there of (2 Timothy 3:5).

We look the part from the surface level but on the inside, there is a great work that needs to be done in us. Most of us have not given God access to do the work that needs to be done. As a result, we keep wandering in the wilderness. We are fooled by the fact that we think because God is using us, if we are doing the work, or going to church that you are right with God. That is deception at its best. You must be processed. Jesus said, "You will know a tree by its fruit (Matthew 7:16)." The purpose is to get you to produce the right fruit which is the fruit of the Spirit (Galatians 5:22-23).

The 3rd scenario showed four examples of being tested in your obedience to God vs. leadership. Oftentimes in the church, you will see where people become entrapped or blinded to making their leader their God. They subconsciously put their leader in God's place. God allows us to be tested in this way to show us whether or not He is really Lord in our lives. Our obedience and the chain of command is always under any circumstance is to put God first. No one can override what God says. That is why we have to be taught proper authority through the eyesight of God.

For example, a child's first line of authority is their father and mother. That is why God commands us to honor them because it is training that teaches them to respect authority, the chain of command, and how to honor God as being first. So even with a child if their parents instruct them to do something, they ought to do it. No one should think or try to override their parent's authority; not grandparents, aunts, uncles, siblings, etc. Understanding that as long as your leader is instructing you according to the Word and way of the Lord, then your leader is pointing you to God. It is when they are not that the issue comes. Paul said follow me as I follow Christ (1 Corinthians 11:1). And to obey God, His word and Spirit is to follow Christ.

ENDING CONCLUSION: "WHERE I WENT WRONG"

I kept making the same mistakes because of my wrong mindset. I did not like receiving correction because I did not like the way it made me feel. I allowed my feelings and emotions to govern me. I lacked in seeking God out for understanding.

WHAT I LEARNED:

God has my best interest at heart so verses me rebelling against the process, I'll obey Him. Process can be defined as a series of action or steps taken in order to achieve a particular end or result.[5] It is best to obey God the first time, or you will find yourself dealing with the same problems years later because you refused to allow God to solve the problem by processing you. God is always trying to work on us because He wants us to be whole in Christ. That is when we are at our best. Will you let God take you through your process? P.S. your test, hardship, temptation, trials, everyday life, is your process, so embrace it.

CHAPTER 4

POURING INTO YOU

Just as God empties you out, He pours into you as well. The emptying out makes room for the pouring in. The more you allow God to empty you, the more He can pour Himself into you. When you look at yourself, can you see God? Do you see a little bit of God or a lot? Have you allowed God to empty you of yourself? Do you continue to allow God to empty you? The more you yield to allowing God to empty you, the more room He has to pour into you. The reality is this; you get as much of God as you want. If you are lacking in God, it is due to ignorance; you are not making Him your number one priority. Being called a Christian does not make you like God, but it is your obedience to die-to-self.

Dying to self is putting away your will and your way of doing things and becoming one with Christ through the Holy Spirit. Often times people or believers confuse or associate being like God with being a Christian, going to church, praying, preaching, and so on. What really makes one like God is having the Spirit of God and allowing the Spirit of God to transform you into being like Christ.

In the book of Genesis, God created mankind (Genesis 1:26-28). He said, "Let us make man in our image, after our likeness." Then in Genesis 2:7 God breathe into man the breath of life and man became a living soul. God created us to be in His image. Image can be defined as the representation of the external form of, and likeness. It can also be defined as the quality or state of having the same characteristics or qualities as.[6] It is impossible to live this out without the Holy Spirit. Without the Holy Spirit, we are dead spiritually. In third John, Jesus talked about a man becoming born again; being born of the water and the Spirit.

Not by works of righteousness which we have done, but according to His mercy he saved us by washing of regeneration and renewing of the Holy Ghost.— Titus 3:5

When God originally created mankind, it was in His image and likeness. The day Adam disobeyed God, he died spiritually. He was no longer connected to God. When Adam was fruitful and multiplied in having children, he was in a state of being degenerated. Degenerated is defined as having lost the physical, mental, or moral qualities considered normal and desirable; showing evidence of decline. It also means an immoral or corrupt person.[7] As a result, all was born into a state of sin and being spiritually detached from God. But now that Jesus has died for us, we are not only forgiven for our sins but reconciled to God's original intent for us being restored to His Image and likeness.

And all things are of God, who hath reconciled us to himself by Jesus Christ, and hath given to us the ministry of reconciliation; To wit, that God was in Christ, reconciling the world unto himself, not imputing their trespasses unto them; and hath committed unto us the word of reconciliation. — 2 Corinthians 5:18-19

That starts when someone not only receives salvation but becomes born again:

Jesus answered Verily Verily I say unto thee, except a man be born of water and of the Spirit he cannot enter into the kingdom of God.—John 3:5

Not by works of righteousness which we have done, but according to his mercy he saved us, by the washing of regeneration, and renewing of the Holy Ghost; —Titus 3:5

Now the water represents the washing of regeneration. Regeneration is being reborn spiritually and renewing. It also can be defined as making like new, to do again, and to restore to existence.[8]

That is what being born again does, it gives us the chance to be and live the way God originally intended for us. This is why we must allow God to pour into us through our yielding and submission to the Holy Ghost. The Holy Spirit comes to lead us and guide us in all truth (John 16:13). The truth is that we were created to be like God. Jesus said the hour is come where God is seeking true worshipers; those that will worship Him in Spirit and in truth (John 4:23).

God wants us serving Him as one being filled with His Spirit which is His image and likeness and in truth knowing who we are in Him. He also wants us to know what we were created to do but most of us are serving Him from a place of brokenness and not wholeness. Brokenness is a beautiful place when it is accompanied with a contrite heart (Psalms 51:17). Contrite means to feel remorseful for wrong doing.[9] When we are in the place of brokenness and have a contrite heart, God can pour Himself into us. When you accept and know what you have been doing, trying is not and has not worked. You need change, you need God. A lot of us find ourselves in a place of brokenness but without having a contrite heart. So, we become like broken cisterns trying to hold God's anointing or Glory, but it keeps leaking out vs. being poured out. In chapter 3, I spoke about the things God subtract from us. Now I will discuss the things God adds to us.

The things God wants to add to us is His love, joy, peace, long suffering, faith, temperance, gentleness, goodness, and meekness this is the fruit of His Spirit (Galatians 5:22-23). Additional things that God wants to give us are strength, grace, anointing, glory, wisdom, knowledge, revelation, prudence, understanding and more. The reason that God pours into us is we're His investment. Investment is the act of putting something in, in order to profit and get something out.[10] God is not adding and pouring things into us just so we can look good, but He wants to be glorified through us. In return, He wants to receive us in the day of judgement. It is a must for us to cooperate with and yield to the Holy Spirit, so we can receive all that God has to pour into us.

ENDING CONCLUSION: "WHERE I WENT WRONG."

The mistake that I made was that I kept interrupting the process in the seasons of my life when God wanted to pour into me. I was connecting myself to the wrong people and things. It caused me to be contaminated and stripped me of my strength and virtue.

WHAT I LEARNED:

I learned in order for God to be seen in or through me, He first has to be in me. I can only reflect what is in me whether it is good or bad. God cannot pour out of me what is not in me. So, if God wants to pour His love or anointing out of me, it first has to be in me. Never settle for just having some of or a little of God when you can have the overflow of God. Remember, you get as much of God as you want and not everybody wants God.

CHAPTER 5

INTIMACY

Intimacy is a close, familiar and usually affection loving personal relationship with another person or group. A close association with or detail knowledge or deep understanding of.[11] This is what God desires from us as believers, to commune with Him through His word and Holy Spirit. Commune is to be in intimate communication or rapport[12]

But he is a Jew which is one inwardly; and circumcision is that of the heart, in the Spirit, and not in the letter; whose praise is not of men but of God— (Roman 2:29)

It is one thing to pray to God. Yet, it is another to be able to commune with Him through prayer or reading His word. We often hear in fellowship service about the importance of praying and reading the word of God. How often are people doing these things because in their hearts they just want to take the time to get to know God in a way that they are communing with Him? Most of us have knowledge and understanding of God, but are we rightly dividing the word of truth (2 Timothy 2: 15)? Jesus asked, "Who do man say that I the son of man am?"

When Jesus came into the coasts of Caesarea Philippi, he asked his disciples, saying, Whom do men say that I the Son of man am? And they said, Some say that thou art John the Baptist: some, Elias; and others, Jeremias, or one of the prophets. He saith unto them, But whom say ye that I am? And Simon Peter answered and said, Thou art the Christ, the Son of the living God. And Jesus answered and said unto him, Blessed art thou, Simon Barjona: for flesh and blood hath not revealed it unto thee, but my Father which is in heaven. And I say also unto thee, That thou art Peter, and upon this rock I will build my church; and the gates of hell shall not prevail against it. And I will give unto thee the keys of the kingdom of heaven: and whatsoever thou shalt bind on earth shall be bound in heaven: and whatsoever thou shalt loose on earth shall be loosed in heaven—Matthew 16:13-19

Even today, Jesus is still asking that question. Ask yourself, do you really know who Christ is or are you going by what you have been taught, heard, or by your own understanding? Jesus then turned to His own and asked, who do you say I am? Jesus is not fooled by who claims to be a Christian vs. who has an intimate relationship with Him. What do you know about God? Jesus told Peter, "Flesh and blood did not reveal this to you but my Father who is in Heaven." Then Jesus said, "Upon this rock I am building my church, and the gate of hell shall not prevail against it." In order for one to know Jesus, God has to reveal it from heaven. It is just like when a man meets a woman and start to get to know her, and he knows people that know her. He can go by what the people who know her tell him about her, or he can go by what she reveals to him and their interaction.

A lot of believers and people are the same way today. They do not know God from a place of communing, they just know what they have been taught. Having a title does not mean you know God. Just ask the religious leaders of Jesus time. One of the quickest ways to examine yourself and where you are at with God in an intimate relationship is to consider how you treat people. When you are close to God, He holds you accountable in how you treat people. I will go more into this in the next chapter. Intimacy is the process that leads to becoming one with God. Jesus prayed in John 17: 3, 20-23.

And this is life eternal, that they might know thee the only true God, and Jesus Christ, whom thou hast sent. Neither pray I for these alone, but for them also which shall believe on me through their word; That they all may be one; as thou, Father, art in me, and I in thee, that they also may be one in us: that the world may believe that thou hast sent me. And the glory which thou gavest me I have given them; that they may be one, even as we are one: I in them, and thou in me, that they may be made perfect in one; and that the world may know that thou hast sent me, and hast loved them, as thou hast loved me.—John 17: 3, 20-23

To be one with God is to be in perfect communion with Him. Oneness is the fact or state of being unified or whole though comprised of two or more parts.[13] To be in a state of wholeness is to return to God's original intent for us when He said let us make man in our image and likeness. Going through the intimacy process is to teach and show you how much you are missing God. The more you get to know and understand God, you are getting to know and understand yourself because you were created to be like God. So, the closer you get to Him which is what you are supposed to reflect, you get to see what is off and missing in you. If you are not living and being who God created you to be, then you are off and not complete. God desires us to be intimate and serve Him from a state of being whole. Whole can be defined as all or entire. It is also being In an unbroken or undamaged state; in one piece, or to be complete in oneself.[14] How many of us can honestly say we are whole? When someone is looking to find fulfillment in a person, title, career, material things, sin, etc., then they are not whole.

The Bible tells us in Act 17:28, "In Him we live and move, and have our being; as certain also of your own poets have said for we are also his off springs." We find ourselves as mankind connecting to things and people to fill voids that will never be fulfilled outside of God, living, and doing what He intended for us. We were created for a purpose and whenever you want to understand how to use or operate something, you look to the owner's manual. For example, when you buy a car, in order to know how to operate and use it correctly, you use the car owner's manual. Yes, we can go to the car salesman to answer some questions, but it is only but so far he can take us. Most people are comfortable knowing some or part of something vs. the whole understanding.

We are the same way when it comes to God. We are okay with going to the 5-fold offices (Apostle, Prophet, Pastor, Teacher, and Evangelist) and finding out part those offices vs. going to the owner's manual which is the bible and seeking God out for ourselves.

So, in return, we never come to the fullness of or whole part of what God purposed for us.

I remember when I reached a wall in my process of being intimate with God. It was because I had some areas that I refused to surrender to God since I did not like being vulnerable. Vulnerable is being able to be easily hurt influenced, or attacked; mentally, physically or emotionally.[15] When it came to surrendering my career, church, children, friendships, etc., I was able to give them to God. However, when it came to allowing God to prepare me to be a wife, that was a struggle for me. I was comfortable doing things my way. It took years for me to learn and see what God wanted me to see in this area of my life. It was not until I got tired of making the same mistakes, being broken and unmarried, that my eyes were open. That's when I started to inquire of the Lord.

I thought I was doing it right until I started examining my results and they were all the same. I failed. I got to see why I was failing with interacting with the opposite sex. It was the wrong way and not according to God's word. I thought that being married would complete me. My motive for wanting to be married was wrong. I had things in me still from my childhood. I had abandonment and rejection issues from my father not being around. There were control and manipulation issues from being raised to be an independent woman. That was my mindset. I knew how to use the way I look to get what I wanted from a man. If he did not do what I wanted him to do, then I was done with him. These were a few issues God had to deliver me from. I had to accept that I did not have it all together. I was willing to allow God to fix and strengthen me where I was weak at. I relied on doing things God's way and came out my place of comfort. If someone is not willing to be vulnerable before God, then their intimacy will be impeded because intimacy is to produce the comfort of not knowing how things are going to turn out. Since I know God, I can trust Him and His process. Paul had to learn this lesson as well.

For this thing I besought the Lord thrice, that it might depart from me. And he said unto me, My grace is sufficient for thee: for my strength is made perfect in weakness. Most gladly therefore will I rather glory in my infirmities, that the power of Christ may rest upon me. Therefore I take pleasure in infirmities, in reproaches, in necessities, in persecutions, in distresses for Christ's sake: for when I am weak, then am I strong.— 2 Corinthians 12:8-10

We have to have the same confidence in God no matter where we fall short. God's grace is enough to complete and make us whole. The intimacy process helps to ease the discomfort, shame, doubt, fears and anything else. Intimacy is the number one-way that God desires to communicate with us. Communicate is imparting or exchanging information or news. It is also the act or process of using words, sounds, signs, or behavior to express or exchange information or to express ideas, thoughts feeling, etc., to someone.[16] When God pours into us, it is an act of intimacy. What is more intimate than God giving us Himself? Understand with intimacy comes accountability.

The Bible teaches us about stewardship. Stewardship is a person who is appointed to be responsible for or manage and maintain.[17] For example, think about a relationship when it comes to a man and a woman. If a man wants to be intimate with a woman, God said that they need to be married first. Why? You will be held accountable in how you treat each other. There are consequences for one's actions, whether good or bad. The same thing applies to God. Are you ready to be responsible for your relationship with God? When He tells and show you things, can He trust you to do the right thing with it? Are you ready to protect your relationship with God from distractions, contamination, perversion, sin, etc.?

An intimate relationship with God is not something to be taken lightly. It has to be treasured. I can speak from experience. I messed up in my relationship with God plenty of times. I put my will above doing things God's way because I got tired of waiting on Him and it led to me falling into sin. In Genesis 12:1-3, God called Abraham to be alone with Him. It was not just faith he had to step out on but trust as well. He did not know where God was taking him, but he trusted Him. It is hard to have an intimate relationship with someone you cannot trust. How can I be vulnerable with someone I cannot trust to protect me and the things I share with them? It is the same with God. Understand and know all relationships need forgiveness and room to grow from mistakes. Consider how God grants the same thing to us.

ENDING CONCLUSION: "WHERE I WENT WRONG"

I did not treasure my relationship with God at all cost. I compromised in my relationship. Neglected it. I took it for granted.

WHAT I LEARNED:

I learned that it should not take the absence of God's presence for me to appreciate what I have. Do not take God's mercy and forgiveness for granted by repeating the same mistakes because you know He is going to forgive you. In the process of doing that, you are digging yourself in a deeper hole. You will feel the chastening of your mistakes. Plus, you do not know if God would grant you another chance. If He does, how many years of suffering will it take until the relationship is restored? That is something to consider.

CHAPTER 6

LEARNING WHAT GOD REQUIRES OF YOU

And that servant, which know his Lord's will, and prepared not himself, neither did according to his will, shall be beaten with many stripes. But he that knew not, and did commit things worthy of stripes, shall be beaten with few stripes. For unto whom so ever much is given of him shall be much required: and to whom men have committed much, of him they will ask the more.—Luke 12:47-48

Require means a need for a particular purpose. It also is to demand as necessary or essential.[18] When God gives someone a title, position, assignment, purpose, etc. there are guidelines He gives them to follow. That is to prevent us from doing things the wrong way.

There is a way that seemeth right unto a man, but the end thereof are the ways of death.—Proverb 14:12

The word of God and the Holy Spirit is our guide especially when we live our life, do ministry, business, raise children, marriage, etc. If we live any other way than how God intends for us to live, then we are doing it the wrong way. As people, we easily tend to lean to our own understanding. We go by how others are doing something as the way of doing things. When God gives us responsibility, He expects us to do things His way. In order for us to find good success in God's eyesight.

This book of the law shall not depart out of thy mouth but thou shalt meditate therein day and night, that thou mayest observe to do according to all that is written there in, for then thou shall make thy way prosperous, and then thou shalt have good success.— Joshua 1:8

God requires more from some people and requires less from others. What God requires from us is based on what He has given us. To whom much is given, much is required (Luke 12:48). Understand that there is a minimal requirement that God expects from every believer.

I *beseech you therefore, brethren, by the mercies of God, that ye present your bodies a living sacrifice, holy, acceptable unto God, which is your reasonable service. And be not conformed to this world: but be ye transformed by the renewing of your mind, that ye may prove what is that good, and acceptable, and perfect, will of God.—Romans 12:1-2*

And Jesus answered him, The first of all the commandments is, Hear, O Israel; The Lord our God is one Lord: And thou shalt love the Lord thy God with all thy heart, and with all thy soul, and with all thy mind, and with all thy strength: this is the first commandment. And the second is like, namely this, Thou shalt love thy neighbour as thyself. There is none other commandment greater than these. —Mark 12:29-31

This is my commandment, That ye love one another, as I have loved you.—John 15:12

But without faith it is impossible to please him: for he that cometh to God must believe that he is, and that he is a rewarder of them that diligently seek him.—Hebrews 11:6

To be holy, transformed, to have faith, and love is something that God is asking from every believer. Why does God require more from some than others? Because God gives us what we need to get done concerning the things He asked us to do. Some people God asks for them to do more so they need more to get it done with and others He gives them a particular task. Whether God gives you much or little, He still expects excellence from you in what He has given you to do. Since you represent Him, whatever He gives you it is to be treated and held in honor. Here are some examples from the people God gave much, a particular task and little to do. When I mention someone having little to do, I am referencing the level of responsibility and not as being unimportant. Whatever God is giving us to do is important. Let's start with David.

And David said to Saul, Let no man's heart fail because of him; thy servant will go and fight with this Philistine. And Saul said to David, Thou art not able to go against this Philistine to fight with him: for thou art but a youth, and he a man of war from his youth. And David said unto Saul, Thy servant kept his father's sheep, and there came a lion, and a bear, and took a lamb out of the flock: And I went out after him, and smote him, and delivered it out of his mouth: and when he arose against me, I caught him by his beard, and smote him, and slew him. Thy servant slew both the lion and the bear: and this uncircumcised Philistine shall be as one of them, seeing he hath defied the armies of the living God. David said moreover, The Lord that delivered me out of the paw of the lion, and out of the paw of the bear, he will deliver me out of the hand of this Philistine. And Saul said unto David, Go, and the Lord be with thee. And Saul armed David with his armour, and he put an helmet of brass upon his head; also he armed him with a coat of mail. And David girded his sword upon his armour, and he assayed to go; for he had not proved it. And David said unto Saul, I cannot go with these; for I have not proved them. And David put them off him. And he took his staff in his hand, and chose him five smooth stones out of the brook, and put them in a shepherd's bag which he had, even in a scrip; and his sling was in his hand: and he drew near to the Philistine. And the Philistine came on and drew near unto David; and the man that bare the shield went before him. And when the Philistine looked about, and saw David, he disdained him: for he was but a youth, and ruddy, and of a fair countenance. And the Philistine said unto David, Am I a dog, that thou comest to me with staves? And the Philistine cursed David by his gods. And the Philistine said to David, Come to me, and I will give thy flesh unto the fowls of the air, and to the beasts of the field. Then said David to the Philistine, Thou comest to me with a sword, and with a spear, and with a shield: but I come to thee in the name of the Lord of hosts, the God of the armies of Israel, whom thou hast defied. This day will the Lord deliver thee into mine hand; and I will smite thee, and take thine head from thee; and I will give the carcases of the host of the Philistines this day unto the fowls of the air, and to the wild beasts of the earth; that all the earth may know that there is a God in Israel. And all this assembly shall know that the Lord saveth not with sword and spear: for the battle is the Lord's, and he will give you into our hands. And it came to pass, when the Philistine arose, and came, and drew nigh to meet David, that David hastened, and ran toward the army to meet the Philistine. And David put his hand in his bag, and took thence a stone, and slang it, and smote the Philistine in his forehead, that the stone sunk into his forehead; and he fell upon his face to the earth. So David prevailed over the Philistine with a sling and with a stone, and smote the Philistine, and slew him; but there was no sword in the hand of David. Therefore David ran, and stood upon the Philistine, and took his sword, and drew it out of the sheath thereof, and slew him, and cut off his head therewith. And when the Philistines saw their champion was dead, they fled. —1 Samuel 17:32-51

When the Philistines came up against Israel, David was the man with the mandate on his life to complete the task. A mandate is an official order or commission to do something. It is an authorization to act given to a representative.[19] David was ready to defeat Goliath with confidence in His God although others doubted him. He did not allow that to stop him because God already trained him with the victory of the bear and lion. It is important to know when God gives you something to do; He backs you up. This is why when Saul gave David his armor to fight, David said, "I have been not proven or tested." Instead, he wanted his staff, shepherd bag, five smooth stones, and slingshot. You have to do things the way God tells you to do it even when it does not make sense. It seemed like the right way to defeat the giant was for Saul to give David his armor. However, that was man's way of doing things. This way leads to the way of death (Proverbs 14:12). Always do things God's way because the end results will be victory. In addition, David ended up getting favor with King Saul because he knew and trusted God by doing it His way. The next two examples are two men God required particular things from in order for them to do what He called them to do. The first example is John the Baptist. God gave him what to do in order for him to be successful.

But the angel said unto him, Fear not, Zacharias: for thy prayer is heard; and thy wife Elisabeth shall bear thee a son, and thou shalt call his name John. And thou shalt have joy and gladness; and many shall rejoice at his birth. For he shall be great in the sight of the Lord, and shall drink neither wine nor strong drink; and he shall be filled with the Holy Ghost, even from his mother's womb. And many of the children of Israel shall he turn to the Lord their God. And he shall go before him in the spirit and power of Elias, to turn the hearts of the fathers to the children, and the disobedient to the wisdom of the just; to make ready a people prepared for the Lord. —Luke 1:13-17

And the same John had his raiment of camel's hair, and a leathern girdle about his loins; and his meat was locusts and wild honey.—Matthew 3:4

He was obedient to the instructions of the Lord. He was successful and completed everything God gave him to do. When God requires things from you, you cannot pick and choose what requirements you want to meet. Let's discuss Samson. God required him to be a Nazarite which is an Israelite who was consecrated to the service of God under vows to abstain from alcohol. They have to let their hair grow, and avoid defilement by contact with corpses[20] (Numbers 6:1-12; Judges 13:4-5).

Now therefore beware, I pray thee, and drink not wine nor strong drink, and eat not any unclean thing: For, lo, thou shalt conceive, and bear a son; and no razor shall come on his head: for the child shall be a Nazarite unto God from the womb: and he shall begin to deliver Israel out of the hand of the Philistines.— Judges 13:4-5

God required Samson to live a certain way in order to be successful at what He wanted him to do. Instead,

Samson brought unnecessary punishment on himself because he told Delilah the secret to his strength (Judges 16:17). She used it against him. You have to be cautious of what and who you give your time and strength to. The very thing that he was anointed to do was taken from him. When we do not do what God requires from us, be prepared for things to be taken away. The next two examples are of women who were given little but important responsibilities. The 1st up is Sarah, Abraham's wife. At first, Sarah doubted what was mandated for her to do which was to become a mother of nations.

Now Sarai Abram's wife bare him no children: and she had an handmaid, an Egyptian, whose name was Hagar. And Sarai said unto Abram, Behold now, the Lord hath restrained me from bearing: I pray thee, go in unto my maid; it may be that I may obtain children by her. And Abram hearkened to the voice of Sarai. And Sarai Abram's wife took Hagar her maid the Egyptian, after Abram had dwelt ten years in the land of Canaan, and gave her to her husband Abram to be his wife. And he went in unto Hagar, and she conceived: and when she saw that she had conceived, her mistress was despised in her eyes. And Sarai said unto Abram, My wrong be upon thee: I have given my maid into thy bosom; and when she saw that she had conceived, I was despised in her eyes: the Lord judge between me and thee.—Genesis 16: 1-5

And God said unto Abraham, As for Sarai thy wife, thou shalt not call her name Sarai, but Sarah shall her name be. And I will bless her, and give thee a son also of her: yea, I will bless her, and she shall be a mother of nations; kings of people shall be of her.— Genesis 17:15-16

It is amazing how even when we doubt, want to throw in the towel, or give up, God throws it back at us. He lets us know, "You are not giving up." There were plenty of times, I wanted to and tried to give up, but God would not let me.

If we believe not, yet he abided faithful: he cannot denial himself.—2 Timothy 2:13

Just because things did not happen according to your plan or when you wanted it to, does not mean it is not going to happen. You need to put your plans down and do things God's way. It does not matter how impossible it seems if God spoke it then it will happen. Your age and weakness are not an excuse before God.

And the Lord visited Sarah as he had said, and the Lord did unto Sarah as he had spoken. For Sarah conceived, and bare Abraham a son in his old age, at the set time of which God had spoken to him. — Genesis 21:1-2

Just because you started off in doubt does not mean you have to end up there.

Through faith also Sara herself received strength to conceive seed, and was delivered of a child when she was past age, because she judged him faithful who had promised. — Hebrews 11:11

Remember, it is your faith that is going to get the job done not your resources. The last woman we will discuss is Queen Vashti. Although God did not give her that position, He allowed it. There is something to be learned through Vashti's mistake. When you are given a responsibility, do it, or it will be taken from you.

On the seventh day, when the heart of the king was merry with wine, he commanded Mehuman, Biztha, Harbona, Bigtha, and Abagtha, Zethar, and Carcas, the seven chamberlains that served in the presence of Ahasuerus the king, To bring Vashti the queen before the king with the crown royal, to shew the people and the princes her beauty: for she was fair to look on. But the queen Vashti refused to come at the king's commandment by his chamberlains: therefore was the king very wroth, and his anger burned in him. Then the king said to the wise men, which knew the times, (for so was the king's manner toward all that knew law and judgment: And the next unto him was Carshena, Shethar, Admatha, Tarshish, Meres, Marsena, and Memucan, the seven princes of Persia and Media, which saw the king's face, and which sat the first in the kingdom;) What shall we do unto the queen Vashti according to law, because she hath not performed the commandment of the king Ahasuerus by the chamberlains? And Memucan answered before the king and the princes, Vashti the queen hath not done wrong to the king only, but also to all the princes, and to all the people that are in all the provinces of the king Ahasuerus. For this deed of the queen shall come abroad unto all women, so that they shall despise their husbands in their eyes, when it shall be reported, The king Ahasuerus commanded Vashti the queen to be brought in before him, but she came not. Likewise shall the ladies of Persia and Media say this day unto all the king's princes, which have heard of the deed of the queen. Thus shall there arise too much contempt and wrath. If it please the king, let there go a royal commandment from him, and let it be written among the laws of the Persians and the Medes, that it be not altered, That Vashti come no more before king Ahasuerus; and let the king give her royal estate unto another that is better than she. And when the king's decree which he shall make shall be published throughout all his empire, (for it is great,) all the wives shall give to their husbands honour, both to great and small. And the saying pleased the king and the princes; and the king did according to the word of Memucan: —Esther 1:10-21

Queen Vashti was requested by the King which was her husband at the time to come before him. He wanted to show her off, but she refused his command. As a consequence of her actions, she was replaced and stripped of her royal estate and it was given to another woman who was better than her. Sometimes we are confused in thinking we cannot be replaced by someone else who is better than us. We cannot afford to think like that. It is important to seek God for the what and the how that He requires from us to be successful at what He has given us.

ENDING CONCLUSION: "WHERE I WENT WRONG"

I had to learn the hard way. For example, God let me know that He did not want me to work for someone else. He wanted me to be an entrepreneur. He gave me confirmations through people or prophesy. Instead of me continuing in my business or entrepreneurship, I let it go. I had the wrong people in my ear, sowing doubt and discouragement. This was from people in leadership. Time again, I just quit working my business. I would pick the business up and then stop because I allowed distractions to sidetrack me. Whether it was people giving me the wrong counsel, or worldly wisdom I listen to them vs. continuing in what God gave me. I was like Peter asking for permission to do the impossible. He started on the water and then started sinking because he took his eyes off Jesus.

And Peter answered him and said, Lord, if it be thou, bid me come unto thee on the water. And he said, Come. And when Peter was come down out of the ship, he walked on the water, to go to Jesus. But when he saw the wind boisterous, he was afraid; and beginning to sink, he cried, saying, Lord, save me. And immediately Jesus stretched forth his hand, and caught him, and said unto him, O thou of little faith, wherefore didst thou doubt?— Matthew 14:28-31

WHAT I LEARNED:

When God gives you something, hold fast to it and keep it between you and Him. Remember, God did not call you to be like others. He calls us to be like who He originally intended for us to be. I also learned to not waste time and energy trying to get people to understand me or what God has given me to do. Just let the fruit speak for itself. Remember, everybody is not living to please God. People will try to discourage you or make something out to be wrong with you because your light shines on what they are supposed to be doing but they are not doing. Just continue in what God gives you, and the rest will speak for itself.

CHAPTER 7

KNOWING WHO YOU ARE

What defines you? Is it your hair, looks, shape, size, color, bank account, possessions, relationship status, degree/level of education, career/job, or title/position? What makes you who you are? What type of person are you? How do you treat people? What is your moral upbringing? Do you have integrity or great character? How do you do things? Again, what makes you who you are? Let's start from the bare essentials. Essentials is defined as being absolutely necessary. It means to be extremely important.[21] If you were to lose everything such as your marriage, house, children, bank account, career/job, hair, figure, possessions, etc. Will you still be who you are? Before answering that question, to be fair, ask yourself this, "Do you find your identity in these things?"

Identity is defined as the fact of being whom or what a person or things is; the distinguishing character or personality of an individual.[22] If a person looks to these things for identity then yes, they would have lost the sense of who they are. Oftentimes, we see and hear about people with this type of mindset. When they're faced with a loss they resort to drugs, alcohol, addictions or worst suicide, etc. If we reexamine the definition of essentials, then we will see that if you were to be stripped of these things, then you would still be who you are. Things/possessions or titles do not make a person who they are. What makes up who you are is your essence because that is your essentials, which is your identity.

Essence is the intrinsic or indispensable quality of something, especially something abstract that determines its character; a property or group of properties of something without which it would not exist or be what it is.[23] This is what makes you who you are. When the essence is lost, you lose who you are. How you treat people, your morals, integrity, and character make up what type of person you are. For example, if you are a nice person then you are nice at all times. You will still be nice even when people are not nice to you. Pressure, test, and trials are a test of what type of person you are. Whether you pass, fail or in progress of a test, God wants us to know what is in us so we can see where we measure at according to His standard or righteousness.

And thou shalt remember all the way which the Lord thy God led thee these forty years in the wilderness, to humble thee, and to prove thee, to know what was in thine heart, whether thou wouldest keep his commandments, or no. And he humbled thee, and suffered thee to hunger, and fed thee with manna, which thou knewest not, neither did thy fathers know; that he might make thee know that man doth not live by bread only, but by every word that proceedeth out of the mouth of the Lord doth man live. —Deuteronomy 8:2-3

Christ is our standard, not the world.

And be not conformed to this world: but be ye transformed by the renewing of your mind, that ye may prove what is that good, and acceptable, and perfect, will of God. —Romans 12:2

The world has their standards, but we are not to live by them. For example the world's way of doing things is to love those who love you, but Jesus said the opposite in Matthew 5:43-47.

Ye have heard that it hath been said, Thou shalt love thy neighbour, and hate thine enemy. But I say unto you, Love your enemies, bless them that curse you, do good to them that hate you, and pray for them which despitefully use you, and persecute you; That ye may be the children of your Father which is in heaven: for he maketh his sun to rise on the evil and on the good, and sendeth rain on the just and on the unjust. For if ye love them which love you, what reward have ye? do not even the publicans the same? And if ye salute your brethren only, what do ye more than others? do not even the publicans so?—Matthew 5:43-47

The word of God teaches us how we ought to think, live, and treat people. If people claim to be a Christian, then they need to reflect the character and integrity of Christ. The word of God hates a lying tongue but how many of us lie on a daily basis? We lie whether it is on taxes, to the government, to children, about age or whatever, this is not acceptable to God. I will go more into this in the next chapter. What is on the inside of you makes up who you are on the outside. Character is the mental and moral qualities distinctive to an individual.[24]

Favour is deceitful, and beauty is vain: but a woman that feareth the Lord, she shall be praised. —Proverb 31:30

This is a verse that I keep in the forefront of my mind as a woman because it is important to me what type of person I am on the inside. I faithfully seek and pray to God concerning what type of person I am and how I treat people. If my outer beauty is brighter than my inner beauty that is a problem. I firmly believe when a person is beautiful on the inside it outweighs how they look on the outside. If all I have is how I look on the outside, but I am empty on the inside, then that is vain beauty. I remember being told I was ugly growing up. So I grew up believing that. As a result, it affected the way I approached relationship and how I acted in them. I believed the only way I could get a man was to use my body because I constantly had men complimenting me on my shape and the way I looked. I still believed I was ugly even when they told me the opposite.

At that time, I did not know that being myself and allowing my inner beauty to show was enough. So I hid it. Instead, I used the way I dressed to show off my body and sex to get a man. Although I was doing that, on the inside it was killing me because it was not working. It did not matter how much I would use my body or have sex it never kept them. The men who saw pass my outer beauty and wanted a relationship, I sabotaged it. I remember coming to a place of being tired of being misused. I was tired of men using me for my body. That was the start of my change. I started to see my inner beauty and remember asking myself, "It is more to me than my body and sex?" It was not until after coming to Christ that God destroyed that insecurity in me. It took time, but God showed me who I was. He started giving me my real identity by showing me all the beauty that I had on the inside. He showed me that being loving, caring, respectful, God-fearing, treating people right, honest, humble, having the fruit of His Spirit, forgiving, merciful, and so on is what makes me and other people beautiful. Who I was and how I was living was contrary to what God created me to be. Who you are vs. who God created you to be will always be contrary to each other. Until who you are, aligns with who God created you to be, you will always have insecurities, voids, unhappiness, and so on.

Behold, what manner of love the Father hath bestowed upon us, that we should be called the sons of God: therefore the world knoweth us not, because it knew him not. Beloved, now are we the sons of God, and it doth not yet appear what we shall be: but we know that, when he shall appear, we shall be like him; for we shall see him as he is. And every man that hath this hope in him purifieth himself, even as he is pure.
—1 John 3:1-3

God created us to be the best we can be. People will not reach greatness until they discover the real them. We will just be living life in fear and as someone who settles. The devil does not want us to know who we are so we can live beneath our privileges. The devil wants to keep us from fulfilling the will and purpose God has for us. It starts with knowing who you are in God. Why? Because one must go to the one who created them and the owner's manual which is the bible to know who they are, their purpose, title, position, possessions, etc. to follow. When someone builds who they are, and their life on things, titles, positions, possessions, talents, gifts, and purpose apart from God or not knowing who they are, the Bible refers this to one building on sand. When the storms of life come, they fall because they built on the wrong foundation.

Therefore whosoever heareth these sayings of mine, and doeth them, I will liken him unto a wise man, which built his house upon a rock: And the rain descended, and the floods came, and the winds blew, and beat upon that house; and it fell not: for it was founded upon a rock. And every one that heareth these sayings of mine, and doeth them not, shall be likened unto a foolish man, which built his house upon the sand: And the rain descended, and the floods came, and the winds blew, and beat upon that house; and it fell: and great was the fall of it. —Matthew 7:24-27

And Jesus answered and said unto him, Blessed art thou, Simon Barjona: for flesh and blood hath not revealed it unto thee, but my Father which is in heaven. And I say also unto thee, That thou art Peter, and upon this rock I will build my church; and the gates of hell shall not prevail against it.—Matthew 16:17-18

The one who builds on what God says and the things that He reveals to them are building on a sturdy, sure foundation that will remain standing through the storms of life. Your true success begins with knowing who you are as a person and living who you were created to be. Many people build a successful life and live based on the world's standards of success. They build themselves and their life but it is a lie. So they are constantly wearing masks not knowing who they are or hiding who they are. As a result, there is no self-fulfillment on the inside. Remember who God created you to be should be our standard in this life. If someone does not know what that is, just look at our ultimate example, Jesus Christ.

ENDING CONCLUSION: "WHERE I WENT WRONG"

I was looking at what and who people said I had to be as my standard. I was not happy. For example, when it came to me being a leader in ministry, my leaders would tell me how I had to talk, look, dress, what I could and could not do. I conformed to that. It caused me to take on the spirit of religion, tradition and the spirit of my leader. As a result, God was not pleased nor was I.

WHAT I LEARNED:

Even when you know who you are, you will still be tested and challenged to see if it is Authentic. Embrace who you are and do not compromise. Knowing who you are, produces a self-fulfillment that cannot be taken away from you. Everything else in life such as relationships, ministry, career, purpose, etc. will come together, produce an understanding and a closer connection or intimacy with God. Watch how the plan of God unfolds for you even more and the dots connect to form the overall picture.

But seek ye first the kingdom of God, and his righteousness; and all these things shall be added unto you. —Matthew 6:33

Knowing who you are is a major part of the will of God for your life. That part connects you to your authority to do the assignments and to walk in who God called you to be.

CHAPTER 8

WALKING IN WHO YOU ARE

Walking in who you are goes beyond having a title or position. A title is a name that describes someone's position or job; the name given to something to identify or describe it.[25] A position is a place where someone or something is located or has been put; an employment for which one has been hired.[26] It is the actual being and doing what is required to fulfill and to live out that title or position. In the previous chapter, I asked about the way you treat people. I also asked about your integrity, title, position, etc. I want to go more into it in this chapter. Knowing who you are is one thing but walking in it is another. How many of us have titles or a position that we are fulfilling the requirements of? To say, "I am a Pastor, Prophet, Teacher, Leader, Entrepreneur, Mother, Father, Christian, etc.," are we doing and living by what is required? Are you fulfilling that title? Or are you just carrying the title or position because it sounds good in conversation because it strokes your ego or makes you look like something before men?

How many of us are parents yet we neglect our children, treat and raise them wrong, curse, talk down to them, make promises and do not keep them, too busy to make quality time for them by talking, listen to them, or do something with them? Yet we say we are mothers or fathers. I have been guilty of some of these things and had to apologize to my children for hurting them. How many of us are married but treat our spouse bad by lying, cheating, disrespecting, not submitting, not loving, not praying, and not making sacrifices for them? Yet we claim to be a wife or husband. It is not the title or position that makes you walk into who you are; it is the act of doing it. We are living in a time where people are great performers and mask wearers. We seek the honor that comes from man and not God.

How can ye believe, which receive honour one of another, and seek not the honour that cometh from God only?—John 5:44

But Jesus said you will know them by their fruit in Matthew 7:16-20.

Ye shall know them by their fruits. Do men gather grapes of thorns, or figs of thistles? Even so every good tree bringeth forth good fruit; but a corrupt tree bringeth forth evil fruit. A good tree cannot bring forth evil fruit, neither can a corrupt tree bring forth good fruit. Every tree that bringeth not forth good fruit is hewn down, and cast into the fire. Wherefore by their fruits ye shall know them.— Matthew 7:16-20

It is not by what they say, do, or how they look. It is by how they live. Do not get me wrong, it is very honorable to have a position or title but remember from chapter 6 there are requirements that come along with that position or title. We see a lot of examples in the world, as well as the bible of people who are in positions, but they disgrace the title or position they have because the way they live their life. How many times do we hear of government officials who are caught up in scandals or corruption instead of them doing the job they were elected to do? People are married but cheat on their spouse. Parents are neglecting their children. Pastors or prophets are bringing shame to their office. Even in the Bible, King Saul feared man. So he disobeyed the instructions and the order that God gave him and blamed the people.

And Samuel said, When thou wast little in thine own sight, wast thou not made the head of the tribes of Israel, and the Lord anointed thee king over Israel?

And the Lord sent thee on a journey, and said, Go and utterly destroy the sinners the Amalekites, and fight against them until they be consumed. Wherefore then didst thou not obey the voice of the Lord, but didst fly upon the spoil, and didst evil in the sight of the Lord? And Saul said unto Samuel, Yea, I have obeyed the voice of the Lord, and have gone the way which the Lord sent me, and have brought Agag the king of Amalek, and have utterly destroyed the Amalekites. But the people took of the spoil, sheep and oxen, the chief of the things which should have been utterly destroyed, to sacrifice unto the Lord thy God in Gilgal And Samuel said, Hath the Lord as great delight in burnt offerings and sacrifices, as in obeying the voice of the Lord? Behold, to obey is better than sacrifice, and to hearken than the fat of rams. —1 Samuel 15:17-22

We have a world full of people like this who do not take accountability for their actions nor the responsibility they were given. The reason we see this is because even from chapter 7, a title or position does not make you who you are. It is your character and morals that make you. Morals can be defined as being concerned with the principles and wrong behavior and the goodness or badness of human character; a person standard of behavior or belief concerning what is and is not acceptable for them to do.[27] When a person has a title or position, if they are corrupt then they will bring dishonor to the position or title they were given. Just like if a person has good character and integrity, they will hold honor to the position or title they were given. Therefore, it is important to live a life of wholeness which means being undivided.[28] Most of us know the right thing to do, but we chose to do wrong. For example, if I am going to claim the title of a Christian then I need to follow Christ by living the way the word of God requires me. Whether we like or accept it, how we are in a time of hardship is a true test of who we really are. But the good news is Jesus came to give us power, truth, and grace.

As many as received him, to them gave he power to become the sons of God, even to them that believe on his name. For the law was given by Moses, but grace and truth came by Jesus Christ.— John 1:12,17

So, we can return to the original intent of who God created us to be, in His Image and likeness.

And God said, Let us make man in our image, after our likeness: and let them have dominion over the fish of the sea, and over the fowl of the air, and over the cattle, and over all the earth, and over every creeping thing that creepeth upon the earth.— Genesis 1:26

Most of the time we are trying to be something we are not or reflecting what we perceive to be acceptable according to society's standard. The sad part is that most people do not want to be the way that God created them, when He created us to be so much better. We rather settle than to rise to greatness. When you are walking in who God created you to be, it is such an indescribable fulfillment.

But the fruit of the Spirit is love, joy, peace, longsuffering, gentleness, goodness, faith, Meekness, temperance: against such there is no law. — Galatians 5:22-23

When you walk in God's character and likeness, it does not matter what position or title you are given. Whether you are a spiritual leader, parent, spouse, government office, CEO, entrepreneur, career, friend, sibling, neighbor, etc. you will bring honor to it. Let's examine an example from the bible of two women, Ruth and Naomi, who were tested through the hardships of life. Naomi's daughter-in-law, Ruth refused to leave her when she was put under pressure of the hardship of losing almost everything. Naomi material possessions as well as her husband and two sons. Instead, Ruth wanted Naomi's God and what Naomi had on the inside of her. Ruth did not judge Naomi based on what she had on the outside which was her title, position, finances, material possession, etc. Ruth seen something greater, she seen the real Naomi. We can see how God rewarded her in return.

Then said Boaz unto his servant that was set over the reapers, Whose damsel is this? And the servant that was set over the reapers answered and said, It is the Moabitish damsel that came back with Naomi out of the country of Moab: And she said, I pray you, let me glean and gather after the reapers among the sheaves: so she came, and hath continued even from the morning until now, that she tarried a little in the house. Then said Boaz unto Ruth, Hearest thou not, my daughter? Go not to glean in another field, neither go from hence, but abide here fast by my maidens: Let thine eyes be on the field that they do reap, and go thou after them: have I not charged the young men that they shall not touch thee? and when thou art athirst, go unto the vessels, and drink of that which the young men have drawn. Then she fell on her face, and bowed herself to the ground, and said unto him, Why have I found grace in thine eyes, that thou shouldest take knowledge of me, seeing I am a stranger? And Boaz answered and said unto her, It hath fully been shewed me, all that thou hast done unto thy mother in law since the death of thine husband: and how thou hast left thy father and thy mother, and the land of thy nativity, and art come unto a people which thou knewest not heretofore. The Lord recompense thy work, and a full reward be given thee of the Lord God of Israel, under whose wings thou art come to trust.—Ruth 2:5-12

We can also learn from Ruth's example of not connecting with people because what they have to offer materially but the value, they can add to the real you. Instead, they make you better as a person, leader, business person, parent, etc., while pushing you closer to God and purpose. Seek to be the best you based on who God called you or created you to be and not how much material possession you can gain. That type of mindset is what the bible refers to as vainglory.

Let us not be desirous of vain glory, provoking one another, envying one another.—Galatians 5:26

Let nothing be done through strife or vainglory; but in lowliness of mind let each esteem other better than themselves. —Philippians 2:3

You can not hide who you are behind a title, position, what you have, or what you do not have. Who are you at the end of the day when it is time to punch out or your assignment is complete? When everybody goes their separate ways and there is no one to perform for and you're alone, who are you? You can only pretend for so long. You may fool some, but there will always be some people who can see through you. People can escape you, but you cannot escape yourself. So why even bother to pretend to be something when you can be the real you?

ENDING CONCLUSION, "WHERE I WENT WRONG"

Although I said I did not care what people thought of me, a part of me did. I was between trying to be me, and what people wanted me to be. I did not know who I was, so I relied on what I thought and what my leaders said about me. That formed my identity.

WHAT I LEARNED:

I learned that I am much happier living to please God vs. living to please myself and people. I learned during discovering who I was that I was not perfect. It was okay for me to make mistakes. I just learned from them. I like being shaped in who God created me to be. It caused me to discover new and cool things about myself that I did not know existed.

CHAPTER 9

LEVEL OF SANCTIFICATION AND REQUIREMENTS

Having therefore these promises, dearly beloved, let us cleanse ourselves from all filthiness of the flesh and spirit, perfecting holiness in the fear of God. —2 Corinthians 7:1

Sanctification is the act or process of being made Holy; the state of proper functioning.[28] Sanctify is to set apart for particular use in a special purpose or work and to make Holy or sacred.[1]

Another part of walking in who you are is walking in sanctification and living a sanctified life. In order to be successful at walking in who you are, it requires staying away from things, places, and people that will hinder, destroy, stagnate or block you from being who you are. These kinds of things will contaminate you. Contaminate is to make impure or unsuitable by contact or mixture with something unclean, bad, etc.[30] This is why sanctification is required and comes in levels. Levels are the height of something.[31] Sanctification is not a onetime thing. It can be seasonal, promotional, basic, and advance.

When one's sanctification is seasonal, it means God will take you through different seasons of sanctification how and when He sees fit. When God has someone in a season of sanctification, it can be short or long depending upon the person's submission, yielding and obedience to the Holy Ghost. This also means a person will be alone a lot during that season. Although God can still have that person connected to people, it will be some distance when He tells them to connect. This also means God wants to bring you into more intimacy.

Promotional sanctification is when a person is going to another level spiritually, naturally, positionally, title, or marriage. These are some examples of promotions. Whatever the promotion is, it's going to require separation. There must be a cutting away, letting go, getting rid of something to make room for the new thing. If not, you will mess up what God has for you. It will cause things to be prolonged. Just be obedient. Yield to the leading of the Holy Spirit and the sanctification process.

Basic sanctification is being called from darkness into light. Whether we realize it or not, to come to salvation you have to come from something. Whatever the hardship that drew you into salvation was your coming from, to come to the better, which is salvation, Hallelujah!

Advance sanctification is to bring you into an office. Examples of offices are the prophet, pastor, king, priest, etc. This level of sanctification is to bring you to a place where God's presence can dwell in you. This is where you can always live and walk in His Spirit. This level requires you to live a life of constant sacrifice. Unlike some other levels of sanctification that requires momentary or seasonal sacrifice, advance sanctification requires your life to be a sacrifice. Jesus said, "No greater love for a man to have for his friend than to lay his life down for his friend."

Greater love has no one than this: to lay down one's life for one's friends.— John 15:13

So, you see, sanctification is required when God wants to take you higher, prepares you for your next, or simply to keep you from getting contaminated. The higher you go, the more sanctification is required.

The more God sanctifies us, the more or longer He can dwell in us. Dwell means to live in or at a specific place.[32] I mentioned in an earlier chapter how God does not just want to visit us but He wants to dwell in us.

He that dwelleth in the secret place of the most High shall abide under the shadow of the Almighty. I will say of the Lord, He is my refuge and my fortress: my God; in him will I trust.— Psalm 91:1-2

Now ye are clean through the word which I have spoken unto you. Abide in me, and I in you. As the branch cannot bear fruit of itself, except it abide in the vine; no more can ye, except ye abide in me. — John 15: 3-4

Just because we experience long or short visitations in God's presence does not mean His Spirit lives with us.

Ye also, as lively stones, are built up a spiritual house, an holy priesthood, to offer up spiritual sacrifices, acceptable to God by Jesus Christ.—1 Peter 2:5

In whom all the building fitly framed together groweth unto an holy temple in the Lord: In whom ye also are builded together for an habitation of God through the Spirit.— Ephesians 2:21-22

The ultimate level of sanctification is to bring you to a place where God's Spirit or presence can dwell in you.

ENDING CONCLUSION: "WHERE I WENT WRONG"

One of the ways that I went wrong was in my thinking. I thought because God had sanctified me that I was done with sanctification. I would fight against God's Spirit in times when He wanted to take me to another level of sanctification. I saw that God was requiring more time from me. I did not understand why which caused me to keep moving every time I would feel bored, anxious, tired of being still or impatient. God had to keep repeating the process or pick up where He left off at until He finished what He wanted to do in me.

WHAT I LEARNED:

It took me constantly making the same mistakes to realize that I had to do things God's way. I realized my way was not working. I had to learn how to press through my flesh and what I was feeling to allow God to complete His work. I also had to learn not to return to the ways God sanctified me from.

CHAPTER 10

GOING HIGHER

The process of sanctification is a stepping stone that helps a person to go higher in God.

Therefore, my beloved brethren, be ye stedfast, unmoveable, always abounding in the work of the Lord, forasmuch as ye know that your labour is not in vain in the Lord.— 1 Corinthians 15:58

This process teaches us that we should never settle or become complacent in God and what He called us to do. Going higher consists of more time with God and being perfected in the state you are in. For example, if a person is at a level 3 in God then that requires the character and fruit of the Spirit of level 3. To keep going to higher levels, it is going to require a higher level of character and the fruit of the Spirit. On level 3 you have a certain amount of patience that is good for that level. On the next level, it is going to require more patience. Your patience has to go deeper. In other words, say your patient when it comes to standing in line waiting to pay for something but when it comes to being patient with the development of others, you have no patience. At level 3, God allowed you to get away with it, but at higher levels, He said, "It is not acceptable." God is requiring more from you. That is a part of you God must perfect. This is a part of discovering more and new things about yourself, purpose, gifts, talents, the good, the bad, and your assignments, etc.

Going higher is a part of becoming the complete you who God created you to be. If we become complacent or refuse to grow, then we are denying our self-completion. So yes, to go higher you must produce more fruit of God's spirit, character, and perfection. You also become closer to being like God and being more intimate with Him. Some may think they can pretend or fool people into believing they are in a higher place in God or position, but your fruit and character will tell on you. If the fruit and character do not match up with your position or title, you must ask yourself, "Did God give me this or man?" You cannot cheat yourself thereby receiving a position by man that is not God approved. The bible says promotion comes from the Lord.

For promotion cometh neither from the east, nor from the west, nor from the south. But God is the judge: he putteth down one, and setteth up another.
— Psalm 75:6-7

The only way you are going higher is if God sees fit to promote you. He determines that by how we go through our process. Even if man gives or gave you a position, it is not official. It will not last and you will not be successful or at peace with it. Your process prepares and makes you ready for the next and what is to come. Along with God's approval, He gives authority and power to do what is required. It is called being equipped. We witness a lot of people who have positions but no authority and power for the position. The reason is that it is not God approved or God prepared. God will not give you something He has not equipped you to handle. If God has given you something, you can handle it. You can do it. You just have to believe and trust God in spite of how you feel or what you think. God does not make mistakes. So, if you feel like you can not do something then that feeling is correct because it is not you doing it but God doing it through you. It is God that worketh in you both to will and do of His good pleasure (Philippians 2:13).

For we are the circumcision, which worship God in the spirit, and rejoice in Christ Jesus, and have no confidence in the flesh —Philippians 3:3.

Higher means rising or extending upward a greater distance. Situated or passing above the normal level, surface base of measurement or elevation.[33] We should constantly strive to grow in God. Going higher reflects one's growth in God. Going higher is about growth. Whether you are a parent, spiritual leader, business owner, entrepreneur, gifted, talented, great character, and have fruits of the Spirit, do not settle. Most importantly as a person, there is always room for growth. Therefore, do not settle for good when you can be great. Do not settle for being great when you can be excellent. When you reach excellence, now maintain it.

ENDING CONCLUSION: "WHERE I WENT WRONG"

When it came to being an entrepreneur, I would start my business but would not see it through. In other words, I did not finish what I started. As a leader when God had me to start a house ministry, I lost track of the vision God gave me. I allowed the wrong counsel in my ear. God had to shut the ministry down to reprocess me and clean up the mess that I made.

WHAT I LEARNED:

When God brings you back to something it is because your assignment is incomplete. I also learned not to allow man to push me before God's time. Even when people offered me platforms, I turned it down because I knew it was not God. One thing that one of my leaders taught me was not to allow people to pimp my gift or anointing and misuse me. Do not rush God. Don't miss God but move with Him!

CHAPTER 11

THE ORIGINAL YOU

Being an original is all about being true to who God made or created you to be. Original is defined as present or existing from the beginning; first or earliest created direct and personally by a particular artist not a copy or imitation.[34] If we take under consideration the definition of original, God is the artist, and we are His masterpiece. He did not create us to be an imitation of someone else but to be like Him.

For we are his workmanship, created in Christ Jesus unto good works, which God hath before ordained that we should walk in them.—Ephesians 2:10

Ephesians 2:10 said it best, we were created to live out the plan He has for us. But we are too busy trying to follow our plan, the world's or man's plan when God's plan is tailored fit for how He created us. We cannot complete one without the other. In other words, to complete the plan, I have to first be what He created me to be. It is like a swimmer trying to be a rapper. Some may ask, "What is wrong with that?" Well, the point I am making is to stay in your lane. Do, be, what and who you were created to do and be. Most importantly, do it the way God wants you to do it. For example, you can have two singers: one a soprano and the other an alto. The alto should not try to sing like a soprano because that is not how they were created to sing and vice versa. Another example, Jeremiah and Ezekiel were both prophets who saw, but God used them differently. God asked Jeremiah what he saw (Jeremiah 1:11-13). The Spirit of the Lord took Ezekiel into visions (Ezekiel 8:3). They did not try to be like each other; they were themselves.

Let's consider flowers. There are plenty of different flowers, too many to name. They all are beautiful, unique and created to serve a particular purpose. That is the same way God created us. We come in different shapes, sizes, and colors. We have different talents, gifts, purposes, and plans but the same end result which is to show forth His Glory. It does not make one better than the other. We all have a purpose. God is not slack when it comes to creativity. Why do you feel the need to copy someone else when you are the only one who can be the best you? No one can be better at being you than you. Do not settle for trying to be like or wanting what someone else has because you do not know what it cost. You will not succeed because you were not created to be like them. Accept you and love yourself. Strive to be the best you can be in God. Do not measure yourself according to people's opinions and standards. God knows what it takes to be the best you so consult with Him concerning your life. Whether it is the way we dress, look, talk, do things, our style, or the way we think, how many of us can say we are an original?

I remember being in high school and my teacher wanting me to do a paper on someone I admired. At that time, I did not admire anyone. The reason was not because there were a lack of great examples. I just did not inspire to be like anyone. Well now, I do admire someone and His name is Jesus. I really inspire to be like Him. He is my inspiration. Another thing I remember during my high school years was being talked about in a good way and sometimes a bad way for being different. I remember one of my friends saying something negative about the way I wore colors together. Then a couple of weeks later, she turned around and tried to do the same thing. I rather get talked about for being me than being like someone else. I rather try to fail at being me than trying to be like someone else.

Before I formed thee in the belly I knew thee; and before thou camest forth out of the womb I sanctified thee, and I ordained thee a prophet unto the nations.
— Jeremiah 1:5

So God created man in his own image, in the image of God created he him; male and female created he them — Genesis 1:27

But ye are a chosen generation, a royal priesthood, an holy nation, a peculiar people; that ye should shew forth the praises of him who hath called you out of darkness into his marvellous light;— 1 Peter 2:9

But now, O Lord, thou art our father; we are the clay, and thou our potter; and we all are the work of thy hand.— Isaiah 64:8

But now hath God set the members every one of them in the body, as it hath pleased him. And if they were all one member, where were the body? But now are they many members, yet but one body. And the eye cannot say unto the hand, I have no need of thee: nor again the head to the feet, I have no need of you. Nay, much more those members of the body, which seem to be more feeble, are necessary: And those members of the body, which we think to be less honourable, upon these we bestow more abundant honour; and our uncomely parts have more abundant comeliness. For our comely parts have no need: but God hath tempered the body together, having given more abundant honour to that part which lacked. That there should be no schism in the body; but that the members should have the same care one for another. And whether one member suffer, all the members suffer with it; or one member be honoured, all the members rejoice with it. Now ye are the body of Christ, and members in particular. And God hath set some in the church, first apostles, secondarily prophets, thirdly teachers, after that miracles, then gifts of healings, helps, governments, diversities of tongues. Are all apostles? are all prophets? are all teachers? are all workers of miracles? Have all the gifts of healing? do all speak with tongues? Do all interpret?. —1 Corinthians 12:18-30

Imitation is a thing intended to simulate or copy something else; something produced as a copy; counterfeit.[35] Tailored is to make or change something especially for a particular person or purpose.[36] Do not go against who God created you to be by trying to be an imitation of someone else. Women you were created to be a woman so do not try to take on the identity of a man. It takes nothing from you by being submissive, taking his lead and instruction. Be a helpmate and feminine, learn and know your role as a woman according to God's standard. The same goes for men that they be who God created them to be.

Be that leader, provider, protector, father, and so on. Do not get caught up in a false perception of what a man is by being prideful or treating a woman less than your equal or her worth. Look to the men and women of the Bible for examples which are Virtuous Women and Men of Valor. Integrity and Godly character is a must. COME FORTH! Together we were created to do this as a team. Both roles are needed (smiley face). Remember, we are the world's standard and an example of how to live life. So do not compromise or water down being you.

ENDING CONCLUSION: "WHERE I WENT WRONG"

I did not understand my worth and strength as being an original. So I would fold into peer pressure, compromise and lessen my worth.

WHAT I LEARNED:

The people who criticized me were the same ones who tried to be like me or secretly admired me. I saw how people took to me because I was me. They wanted to glean or copy me. I learned that people will criticize what they fear, threatened by, or do not understand. Still be you and aim to make God proud.

CHAPTER 12

REPEAT

Repeat means to do something again once or a number of times.[37] We end up repeating things when we try to rush, skip, miss, or do not do it the right way the first time. We repeat the process of seasons God has for us so He takes us through the process again. Why? Because there is more, He wants to add to us or something we lost along the way. Do not see 'repeat' as a bad thing but as a beautiful thing. It is God's way of saying, "I want you to get everything that I have to offer you. You will be a finished work of my hands." Plus, it is Him giving us time to get things right before Jesus returns. Once Jesus comes again, it will be too late. God cannot help you anymore. He now has to deal and judge us according to whatever state we are in. I do not know about you, but I do not want to hear, "Depart from me you workers of iniquity. I never knew you (Matthew 7:23)."

So, I rather let God work on me now. Although I always thought this way, my actions did not line up. In fact, I would get tired of being processed, waiting on God and doing things His way. God still being Himself corrected me anyways because He loves me despite of how I responded to Him. It caused me to come to a place of maturity where I was able to appreciate the process, correction, waiting and so on. I saw the mess I made doing things my way. I had to turn to God asking for His help to clean up my mess. Guess what? His help is your process. "You're welcome," says God. Go through it. Allow God to help you by doing things His way. When you find yourself in a season of 'repeat' be thankful because God is giving you a gift, called 'get it right.' Go through your season with joy.

My brethren, count it all joy when ye fall into divers temptations; Knowing this, that the trying of your faith worketh patience. But let patience have her perfect work, that ye may be perfect and entire, wanting nothing. If any of you lack wisdom, let him ask of God, that giveth to all men liberally, and upbraideth not; and it shall be given him. — James 1:2-5

When you do not know how to go through, ask God for wisdom on how to go through. Know that you need His process and correction for your own good.

ENDING CONCLUSION: "WHERE I WENT WRONG"

I did not realize that I was in a season of repeat, so I kept making the same mistakes. I was yielding to my flesh, emotions, and my way of doing things. I did not prepare myself to go through.

WHAT I LEARNED:

You can prepare yourself to go through your season of 'repeat' by strengthening yourself spiritually and mentally. Fasting, praying, reading, meditation on the Word, praise, and thanksgiving are your weapons to help you pass the test. So, use them. Soldiers do not go to battle without their uniforms and weapons. Neither shall you. Put on the full armor of God because it is your uniform. Also, use the weapons that I mentioned.

Finally, my brethren, be strong in the Lord, and in the power of his might. Put on the whole armour of God, that ye may be able to stand against the wiles of the devil. For we wrestle not against flesh and blood, but against principalities, against powers, against the rulers of the darkness of this world, against spiritual wickedness in high places. Wherefore take unto you the whole armour of God, that ye may be able to with-

stand in the evil day, and having done all, to stand. Stand therefore, having your loins girt about with truth, and having on the breastplate of righteousness; And your feet shod with the preparation of the gospel of peace; Above all, taking the shield of faith, wherewith ye shall be able to quench all the fiery darts of the wicked. And take the helmet of salvation, and the sword of the Spirit, which is the word of God: Praying always with all prayer and supplication in the Spirit, and watching thereunto with all perseverance and supplication for all saints.—Ephesians 6:10-18

Use what God has given you so that you may be victorious. You are a conqueror and overcomer through Jesus Christ.

I hope this book blessed you and made you better. Feel free to read it again and learn something new. God Bless!

ABOUT THE AUTHOR

Shardell Martin is a God-fearing woman, who is a mother of two beautiful children, Sabmier and Saige. She comes from a large family of seven siblings and from a single parent home. She has been on fire and dedicated to the Lord since April 2009. That's when she got saved and filled with the Holy Spirit. She is a purpose driven woman, who loves helping and building up people. Not only is she a voice that speaks the heart and mind of God, she is also a leader and entrepreneur. She is a firm believer of living a life that reflects and glorifies God. She knows her mission is to show and point people back to God, His will, righteous alignment, and good stewardship in every area of life. She knows God has chosen, prepared, equipped, and bestowed His wisdom upon her to be a catalyst and a solution for change. It's been and is a process; she's well prepared and ready to travel.

Shardell is no stranger to carrying her cross. She knows what it is to walk away from a career, family, friend, opportunities, comfort, endure hardship, to wait on the Lord. She is obedient to the call and will of God. God has raised her up not only to be His mouthpiece to nations but to be a Godly example that points His people back to Jesus Christ as the standard.

It has not been and is not an easy cup to drink, but God has equipped and graced her to do it.

Her greatest accomplishment will be all that God has predestined her to be. She is a good steward over what God has entrusted in her care. One day she will hear, "Well done my good and faithful servant. You may enter the joy of the Lord."

REFERENCES

1. "Sanctify." Merriam-Webster.com. Accessed December 13, 2018. https://www.merriam-webster.com/dictionary/sanctify.

2. "Empty." Merriam-Webster.com. Accessed December 13, 2018. https://www.merriam-webster.com/dictionary/empty.

3. "Motive." Merriam-Webster.com. Accessed December 13, 2018. https://www.merriam-webster.com/dictionary/motive.

4. "Intention." Merriam-Webster.com. Accessed December 13, 2018. https://www.merriam-webster.com/dictionary/intention.

5. "Process." Merriam-Webster.com. Accessed December 13, 2018. https://www.merriam-webster.com/dictionary/process.

6. "Image." Merriam-Webster.com. Accessed December 14, 2018. https://www.merriam-webster.com/dictionary/image.

7. "Degeneration." Merriam-Webster.com. Accessed December 14, 2018. https://www.merriam-webster.com/dictionary/degeneration.

8. "Regeneration." Merriam-Webster.com. Accessed December 14, 2018. https://www.merriam-webster.com/dictionary/regeneration.

9. "Contrite." Merriam-Webster.com. Accessed December 14, 2018. https://www.merriam-webster.com/dictionary/contrite.

10. "Investment." Merriam-Webster.com. Accessed December 14, 2018. https://www.merriam-webster.com/dictionary/investment.

11. "Intimacy." Merriam-Webster.com. Accessed December 15, 2018. https://www.merriam-webster.com/dictionary/intimacy.

12. "Commune." Merriam-Webster.com. Accessed December 15, 2018. https://www.merriam-webster.com/dictionary/commune.

13. "Oneness." Merriam-Webster.com. Accessed December 16, 2018. https://www.merriam-webster.com/dictionary/oneness.

14. "Whole." Merriam-Webster.com. Accessed December 16, 2018. https://www.merriam-webster.com/dictionary/whole.

15. "Vulnerable." Merriam-Webster.com. Accessed December 16, 2018. https://www.merriam-webster.com/dictionary/vulnerable.

16. "Communicate." Merriam-Webster.com. Accessed December 16, 2018. https://www.merriam-webster.com/dictionary/communicate.

17. "Stewardship." Merriam-Webster.com. Accessed December 16, 2018. https://www.merriam-webster.com/dictionary/stewardship.

18. "Require." Merriam-Webster.com. Accessed December 16, 2018. https://www.merriam-webster.com/dictionary/require.

19. "Mandate." Merriam-Webster.com. Accessed December 16, 2018. https://www.merriam-webster.com/dictionary/mandate.

20. "Nazarite." Merriam-Webster.com. Accessed December 16, 2018. https://www.merriam-webster.com/dictionary/nazarite.

21. "Essential." Merriam-Webster.com. Accessed December 16, 2018. https://www.merriam-webster.com/dictionary/essential.

22. "Identity." Merriam-Webster.com. Accessed December 16, 2018. https://www.merriam-webster.com/dictionary/identity.

23. "Essence." Merriam-Webster.com. Accessed December 16, 2018. https://www.merriam-webster.com/dictionary/essence.

24. "Character." Merriam-Webster.com. Accessed December 16, 2018. https://www.merriam-webster.com/dictionary/character.

25. "Title." Merriam-Webster.com. Accessed December 16, 2018. https://www.merriam-webster.com/dictionary/title.

26. "Position." Merriam-Webster.com. Accessed December 16, 2018. https://www.merriam-webster.com/dictionary/position.

27. "Morals." Merriam-Webster.com. Accessed December 17, 2018. https://www.merriam-webster.com/dictionary/morals.

28. "Wholeness." Merriam-Webster.com. Accessed December 17, 2018. https://www.merriam-webster.com/dictionary/wholeness.

29. "Sanctification." Merriam-Webster.com. Accessed December 17, 2018. https://www.merriam-webster.com/dictionary/sanctification.

30. "Contaminate." Merriam-Webster.com. Accessed December 17, 2018. https://www.merriam-webster.com/dictionary/contaminate.

31. "Level." Merriam-Webster.com. Accessed December 17, 2018. https://www.merriam-webster.com/dictionary/level.

32. "Dwell." Merriam-Webster.com. Accessed December 17, 2018. https://www.merriam-webster.com/dictionary/dwell.

33. "Higher." Merriam-Webster.com. Accessed December 17, 2018. https://www.merriam-webster.com/dictionary/higher.

34. "Original." Merriam-Webster.com. Accessed December 18, 2018. https://www.merriam-webster.com/dictionary/original.

35. "Imitation." Merriam-Webster.com. Accessed December 18, 2018. https://www.merriam-webster.com/dictionary/imitation.

36. "Tailored." Merriam-Webster.com. Accessed December 18, 2018. https://www.merriam-webster.com/dictionary/tailored.

37. "Repeat." Merriam-Webster.com. Accessed December 18, 2018. https://www.merriam-webster.com/dictionary/repeat.

INDEX

A

abandonment, 33

Abraham, 1, 7–8, 36, 47

accountability, 35, 65

alcohol, 45, 54

anointing, 26–27, 80

apostles, 3, 32, 85

armour, 42, 89

authority, 13–14, 19, 61, 78

B

battle, 43, 89

believers, 1, 5, 7, 28, 30, 39–40, 91

brokenness, 25–26

business, 39, 50, 79

C

chain, 19

character, 53–54, 56, 65, 67, 76–77, 79, 96

children, 18, 24, 33, 39, 44–46, 53, 56, 63–64

church, 2–4, 7, 9–10, 14, 16, 19, 23, 29–30, 33, 60, 85

comfort, 34, 91

compromise, 61, 86

D

disobedient, 45

distractions, 35, 50

dreams, 10–11

E

emotions, 20, 89

entrepreneur, 50, 62, 67, 79, 91

essentials, 53–54, 95

evil, 56

F

Fasting, 89

flesh, 29–30, 60, 71, 75, 78, 89

forgive, 16, 36

fruit, 17–19, 26, 51, 58, 63–64, 67, 74, 76–77, 79

fulfillment, 32

G

gates, 29–30, 60

gifts, 59, 77, 80, 82, 85, 88

glory, 26, 31, 34, 82

governments, 56, 85

grace, 26, 34, 66, 68

growth, 79

H

hardship, 12, 21, 66–67, 73, 91

hate thine enemy, 56

heart, 15, 20, 28–29, 41, 45, 48, 91

heaven, 29–30, 56, 60

Holy Spirit, 5, 15–16, 23, 25–26, 28, 39, 73, 91

honour, 8, 63, 84–85

humiliation, 14

hurt, 3, 14, 17, 33

I

identity, 54, 70, 85, 96

ignorance, 7, 22

image, 16–17, 23–25, 31, 66, 84, 93

impartation, 4

infirmities, 34

iniquity, 8, 87

insecurities, 58

instructions, 45, 64, 85

integrity, 53–54, 56, 62, 66, 86

intention, 15, 93

intimacy, 28, 30, 34–35, 61, 72, 94

K

kingdom, 3, 24, 29, 49, 61

knowledge, 26, 28–29, 68

L

leadership, 5, 13–16, 19, 50

life, 3–4, 9–10, 23, 27, 31, 33, 39, 43, 59–61, 64, 66–67, 73, 83, 91

lifestyle, 1, 7

loving, 58, 63

M

manipulation, 15

marriage, 39, 53, 72

meekness, 18, 26, 67

mercy, 23, 25, 36, 39

mess, 72, 79, 88

mindset, 34, 54, 69

miracles, 85

mother, 19, 46–47, 62–63, 91

motive, 15, 33, 93

O

obedience, 5, 19, 22, 72

P

parents, 9, 19, 63–64, 67, 69, 79

patience, 76–77, 88

peace, 18, 26, 67, 78, 90

permission, 14, 51

perseverance, 90

person, 12, 17, 28, 32, 35, 53–55, 57, 60, 65–66, 69, 72, 76, 79

possessions, 53, 59

pouring, 22, 26

power, 18, 34, 44, 66, 78, 89

praise, 28, 89

praying, 23, 29, 63, 89–90

process, 7, 9–11, 18, 20–21, 27, 30, 33–36, 71, 75–76, 78, 87–88, 91, 93

promises, 63, 71

promotions, 72, 77

prophets, 29, 32, 62, 64, 73, 82, 84–85

R

reapers, 68

regeneration, 23, 25, 94

relationship, 35–37, 57, 61

result, 4, 14, 18, 20, 24, 57, 60–61, 82

revelation, 11, 26

righteousness, 1, 3, 23, 25, 55, 61, 90

S

sacrifices, 63, 65, 73

salvation, 24, 73, 90

sanctification, 71–73, 75–76, 97

Sanctify, 1–2, 7, 71, 93

scenario, 13–19

season, 7, 14, 27, 72, 88–89

seasonal, 72

servant, 38, 68, 92

sex, 57–58

shame, 34, 64

sin, 7, 24, 32, 35–36

spiritual wickedness, 89

strength, 26–27, 34, 46, 48, 86

stripes, 38

submission, 13–15, 25

supplication, 90

sword, 42–43, 90

T

teach, 2, 4, 12, 31

time, 2–5, 8, 11, 14–16, 20, 46, 50, 57–58, 63, 66, 69, 75–76, 80, 83, 87 tongues, 56, 85

trials, 14, 21, 54

trust, 6, 34–36, 68, 74

truth, 2, 4, 25, 29, 66, 90

U

understanding, 11–12, 19–20, 26, 28–30, 32, 39, 61

unforgiveness, 17

unhappiness, 58

V

vain, 56, 76

vainglory, 69

Vashti, Queen, 48–50

victory, 43–44

voice, 11, 46, 65, 91

W

weakness, 34, 47

weapons, 89

wholeness, 25, 31, 66, 96

wilderness, 10, 17–18, 55

wisdom, 26, 45, 88, 91

word, 2–5, 11, 15–17, 20, 24, 28–29, 31, 33, 35, 55–56, 74, 77, 79, 82, 89–90

world, 24, 31, 40, 55, 64–65, 82, 86, 89

www.ingramcontent.com/pod-product-compliance
Lightning Source LLC
Chambersburg PA
CBHW052100110526
44591CB00013B/2288